Parables from The Fishin' Hole

Volume Two

Study Notes by
Mary Guenther

Participant's Guide

Published by

A division of Thomas Nelson Publishers

Copyright © 2001 by Thomas Nelson Publishers

Printed in the United States of America
ISBN 0-8499-8965-5

For Information
Call Thomas Nelson Publishers 1-800-251-4000

Table of Contents

About the Author

Mary Guenther is a freelance writer living in Nashville, Tennessee. She contributed the character sketches for *The Women of Faith Study Bible,* and co-authored *The Bedtime Bible* for children. In her former position as manager of book publishing for Promise Keepers, she was responsible for numerous publications, including the men's video retreat kit, *Face to Face, An Encounter with Christ*. She has written and edited numerous EZ Lesson Plans for Thomas Nelson Multimedia.

Parables from The Fishin' Hole

Volume 2

Session One
The Big House

The Big House
(A Study on Humility)

LUKE 14:8-11

"When you are invited by anyone to a wedding feast, do not sit down in the best place, lest one more honorable than you be invited by him; and he who invited you and him come and say to you, 'Give place to this man,' and then you begin with shame to take the lowest place. But when you are invited, go and sit down in the lowest place, so that when he who invited you comes he may say to you, 'Friend, go up higher.' Then you will have glory in the presence of those who sit at the table with you. For whoever exalts himself will be humbled, and he who humbles himself will be exalted."

There are times when we can study a character trait best by considering its opposite. "The Big House" gives us just that opportunity. We can't say that Barney is humble, but we can say he is, well. . .just Barney.

How would you define the word "humility"?

_____

_____

PSALM 25:9

The humble He guides in justice,
And the humble He teaches His way.

According to the scripture passage above, what are some benefits of humility?

_____

_____

_____

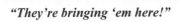

"They're bringing 'em here!"

> Build me a son, O Lord, who will be strong enough to know when he is weak, and brave enough to face himself when he is afraid; one who will be proud and unbending in honest defeat, and humble and gentle in victory.
> —General Douglas MacArthur[1]

3

Have you prayed for God to make you humble?
❏ **Often**　　　❏ **Sometimes**　　　❏ **Never**
Why or why not?

_____

_____

_____

A Chance to Shine

Life provides many opportunities to display humility—usually in the form of challenges (problems). Barney seizes a unique opportunity to impress others with his skills.

Barney: Well, well, well. So we're gonna have visitors.
Andy: Mmm. Looks like.
Barney: Well, I tell you something. Those two hoods are in fer a big surprise. They're gonna come in here expecting some small town, two-bit lockup, a rinky-dink clubhouse. Well, they're gonna find out differently.
Andy: What've you got in mind?
Barney: I'm gonna show 'em we're on our toes out here, that the Mayberry jail beats any big time pen they've ever served time in!

The first step in humility is making an accurate assessment of our strengths and weaknesses to deal with any situation.

What is wrong with Barney's approach?

_____

_____

"Whistle. . ."

"Obey all the rules. . ."

Listen carefully when the people who know you best say something is a bad idea.[3]

Gathering Resources

The second step in humility is finding ways to cover our weak spots. If we've made a mistake in our initial assessment, we are likely to build on a shaky foundation. Let's consider Barney's next move. . .

> **Barney**: Pretty sharp, huh? (meaning Gomer)
> **Andy**: Gomer? Workin' round the jailhouse? Not Gomer.
> **Barney**: Andy, I know he's green, he's raw, but I can bring him along. I got him on a crash program. He's learned a lot from me already.
> **Andy**: Not Gomer.
> **Barney**: You watch this. Just watch.

Why do you think Barney refused to heed Andy's advice?

_____

_____

Why do you think Andy let Barney hire Gomer?

_____

_____

If you were Andy, would you have gone along with Barney's plan?
❑ **Yes**　　❑ **No**　　❑ **Maybe**
Why or why not?

_____

_____

_____

He has shown you, O man, what is good; and what does the LORD require of you but to do justly, to love mercy, and to walk humbly with your God?

Micah 6:8

Your Attitude's Showing

Barney is funny because he acts like we do—but "in spades". If fools rush in where angels fear to tread, Barney jumps in with both feet!

With the crooks:

Barney: Now men, there are a few things we ought to get straight right at the start to avoid any grief later on. Here at "The Rock" we have two basic rules. Memorize them so that you can say them in your sleep. The first rule is, "Obey all the rules!" The second rule is "Do not write on the walls, as it takes a lot of work to erase writing off of walls."

With Andy and Gomer:

[on roof]
Andy: Look at all this Christmas mess. Barn, You're supposed to clean this up.
Barney: I will. Right now there's more important things to do. (to Gomer) You're supposed to be watching!

"Gomer, you're supposed to be watching!"

How did each of the following characters respond to Barney's sense of importance?

The crooks _____

Andy _____

Gomer _____

Can you recall a time when your need to impress someone got in the way of solving a problem? (If so, share briefly.)

_____

_____

6

Predictably, Barney failed to impress the very people he had hoped to.

Tiny: I don't get it, Rock—you going along with that hick deputy.
Rock: Just playin' it smart, Tiny. Let him think he's a big shot. Lead him on far enough and that hick deputy's gonna be our free pass outa here.

Plainclothes detective: Well deputy, I hope you realize what you've done. Instead of capturing two more, you've now lost all four.

Meanwhile, Andy kept bailing Barney out of trouble.

Would you say that Andy showed humility in his role as Mayberry sheriff?
❑ Yes   ❑ No   ❑ Maybe
Why or why not?

_____

_____

_____

In our culture, many people think humility is the same as humiliation.
Are they?   ❑ Yes   ❑ No   ❑ Maybe
Why do you think so?

_____

_____

_____

"You goin' along with that hick deputy?"

7

Do you think that Barney's pride or humility led to the plainclothesmen's low opinion of him? ❑ **Pride**   ❑ **Humility** *Why?*

_____

_____

_____

"Somethin's going on down there!"

Mistakes Have Value

Even when our pride causes us to fail miserably, we can learn from our mistakes and grow more humble. Andy generously gave Barney an escape route to save face.

Andy: (bringing back the crooks). Great work, **Barney**: Your scheme worked! Didn't even have to fire a shot. The lightbulbs did the trick.
Barney: Lightbulbs?
Andy: I'll explain it all to you later. First we'd better notify the state police. Great work, Barn.

But poor Barney misses his cue—again—and continues in his pride.

Barney: Now men, I hope this has taught you a lesson.

Why do you think Barney reacted that way?

_____

_____

Have you ever hung on to your pride because it was too embarrassing to admit a mistake?

_____

_____

_____

Now that you've considered the benefits of humility, are you willing to pray for God to make you more humble?

❏ **Yes**   ❏ **No**   ❏ **Maybe**

Why or why not?

_____

_____

_____

"You've now lost all four!"

Jet lag is nature's way of making you look like your passport photo.[6]

To hide the shameful fact that his father had been hanged for cattle stealing, a lawyer rewrote his own family history thus: Father died while taking part in a public ceremony when the platform gave way.

–Msgr. Arthur Tonne[7]

HUMILITY LITMUS TEST

Read aloud and briefly discuss each quote below. Check the appropriate box, noting how each applies to your own personal life experience.

Sense shines with a double luster when set in humility.   –William Penn
❏ Applies   ❏ Sometimes Applies   ❏ Does Not Apply

A mountain shames a molehill until they are both humbled by the stars.[9]
❏ Applies   ❏ Sometimes Applies   ❏ Does Not Apply

The man who is to take a high place before his fellows must take a low place before his God[10]
❏ Applies   ❏ Sometimes Applies   ❏ Does Not Apply

It is always the secure who are humble. –G. K. Chesterton[11]
❏ Applies   ❏ Sometimes Applies   ❏ Does Not Apply

He who walks in humility has clear thoughts. –Hasidic saying[12]
❏ Applies   ❏ Sometimes Applies   ❏ Does Not Apply

Be proud, but not boastful. Be strong, but not inflexible. Be brave, but not reckless[13]
❏ Applies   ❏ Sometimes Applies   ❏ Does Not Apply

Everybody can be great . . . because anybody can serve. You don't have to have a college degree to serve. You don't have to make your subject and verb agree to serve. You only need a heart full of grace. A soul generated by love.   –Martin Luther King, Jr.[14]
❏ Applies   ❏ Sometimes Applies   ❏ Does Not Apply

Don't be afraid to say: "I don't know." "I made a mistake." "I need help." "I'm sorry."
❏ Applies   ❏ Sometimes Applies   ❏ Does Not Apply

1. *Which of the above quotes is closest to your own idea of humility? Why?*

_____

_____

_____

2. *Which presents the greatest challenge to you? Why?*

_____

_____

_____

Humility Action Points

1. Lie on your back and look at the stars.
2. Every person that you meet knows something you don't; learn from them.
3. When playing games with children, let them win.
4. Hire people smarter than you.
5. When someone offers you a breath mint, take it.

Personal Notes

_____

_____

_____

_____

_____

_____

_____

_____

_____

_____

_____

_____

_____

_____

_____

_____

_____

_____

_____

_____

_____

_____

[1] H. Jackson Brown, Jr. and Hy Brett, *A Book of Love for My Son* (Nashville: Rutledge Hill Press, 2001)

[2] Frank S. Mead, *12,000 Inspirational Quotations* (Springfield, MA: Federal Street Press, 1965)

[3] Jackson Brown, Jr., Paula Y. Flautt, and Kim Shea, *A Book of Love for My Daughter* (Nashville: Rutledge Hill Press, 2001)

[4] H. Jackson Brown, Jr. and Hy Brett, *A Book of Love for My Son* (Nashville: Rutledge Hill Press, 2001)

[5] Frank S. Mead, *12,000 Inspirational Quotations* (Springfield, MA: Federal Street Press, 1965)

[6] *Ibid.*

[7] Lowell D. Streiker, *Nelson's Big Book of Laughter* (Nashville: Thomas Nelson, 2000)

[8] Jackson Brown, Jr., Paula Y. Flautt, and Kim Shea, *A Book of Love for My Daughter* (Nashville: Rutledge Hill Press, 2001)

[9] *Ibid.*

[10] *Ibid.*

[11] Rudolf Flesch, *The New Book of Unusual Quotations* (New York: Harper & Row, 1966)

[12] *Ibid.*

[13] Jackson Brown, Jr., Paula Y. Flautt, and Kim Shea, *A Book of Love for My Daughter* (Nashville: Rutledge Hill Press, 2001)

[14] H. Jackson Brown, Jr. and Hy Brett, *A Book of Love for My Son* (Nashville: Rutledge Hill Press, 2001)

Parables from The Fishin' Hole

Volume 2

Session Two
The Darlings are Coming

The Darlings are Coming
(A Study on Self-control)

JAMES 1:22-25
But be doers of the word, and not hearers only, deceiving yourselves. For if anyone is a hearer of the word and not a doer, he is like a man observing his natural face in a mirror; for he observes himself, goes away, and immediately forgets what kind of man he was.

How would you define the word "self-control"?

_____

_____

_____

> No man is free who is not master of himself.
>
> **–Epictetus**[1]

"She's always good fer 11 hats full."

How about those Darlings? Did you find them appealing? Few of us would disagree. Americans like folks who "beat the system." From Rambo to Bonnie and Clyde, they fill our movie screens and TV prime time. You could say we're all a bunch of non-conformist "wannabes." What's wrong with that? Well, for starters, so were Adam and Eve. Sadly, we're more inclined to spend energy finding ways to bend the rules than we are on growing in the likeness of Jesus. But the good news is that God knows that and is ready to help us as soon as we are ready to ask!

PHILIPPIANS 1:6
Being confident of this very thing, that He who has begun a good work in you will complete it until the day of Jesus Christ.

"Rules Are Made to be Broken."

It's true that sometimes the laws in Mayberry seem pointless and outdated. That's probably why Mr. Darling didn't take Andy seriously at their first encounter.

> **Andy:** Mr. Darling, as sheriff, there's something I'd like to say to you. It's about parking your truck here in front of our memorial trough and filling your radiator out of it.
> **Briscoe Darling:** What'd ye have in mind?
> **Andy:** Well, the fact is, you're breaking two city ordinances. It's against the law to park here, and you're dippin' your hat into the horse trough. . . That's for horses only.
> **Brisco:** There ain't a horse in sight. But if one comes along, I'll give 'im right of way.

Are there any rules or laws that you think are pointless, such as speed limits, or dress codes?

_____

_____

_____

How do you relate to these kinds of rules/laws?
❑ **Obey anyway**   ❑ **Disobey**   ❑ **Depends on how I feel**

_____

_____

_____

Is there any consequence in ignoring something we consider insignificant? (Hint: What if everybody did?)

_____

_____

"All together ag'in."

"Starlings? At this time of year?"

The Circle of Influence Grows

Briscoe has a different reaction when Charlene challenges *his* rules and gives in to *her* feelings.

Briscoe: That's enough, Charlene. Back in the truck.
Charlene: Oh Pa, can't I even look at the pretty man?
Briscoe: Back in the truck!

First he rationalizes her behavior:

Outside of me and her brothers, there ain't no fellas left in the mountains to play with her. You mighty refreshing to her.

Then he blames Andy:

Briscoe: Their betrothal's been pledged since they was five. So don't go takin' any fancies for her.
Andy: Well, that's the furthest thing from my mind.
Briscoe: Your words say "no", but your eyes say, "Yes".
Andy: Believe me, the thought never entered my mind.

We do the same things when we lack self-control or see it in our loved ones. Perhaps it's the weather, not enough sleep, if only he/she would act differently. . . You fill in the blanks.

Can you think of a specific behavior you have that you blame on "circumstances"?

_____

Is there some behavior you blame on "other people"?

_____

Wisdom does not show itself so much in precept as in life--in a firmness of mind and mastery of appetite. It teaches us to do as well as talk, and to make our actions and words all of a color.

–Seneca[3]

17

Those who forsake the law praise the wicked, But such as keep the law contend with them.

Evil men do not understand justice, But those who seek the LORD understand all.

Proverbs 28:4-5

Do you think Briscoe's casual attitude toward the law affected Charlene's behavior? ☐ **Yes** ☐ **No** ☐ **Maybe**
Why or why not?

_____

_____

No One Will Know

The plot thickens. This time Briscoe knows the law, but adds deception to the mix.

> **Briscoe:** Who do I see about getting' a room to bed down?
> **John Masters:** I can arrange an accommodation. Are you alone?
> **Briscoe:** Just me and my luggage.
> **John:** A single room with bath is $2.50 a night; a single room without bath is $1.75.
> **Briscoe:** Just give me $1.75 worth.
> **John:** I have a nice room for you right up in front.
> **Briscoe:** I'd ruther have something as far back as I kin git.

Can you think of some reasons why Briscoe didn't tell the truth? [Lack of money; habit; didn't agree with the rules; pride about not taking "charity"]

_____

_____

If we're honest, all of us have been tempted to do the same in similar circumstances. In the short run, we tell ourselves our "little white lie" won't hurt anybody.

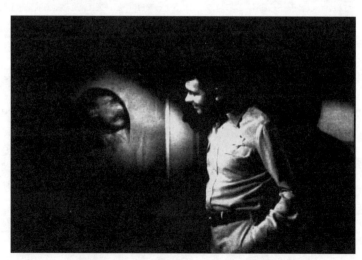

"What number did we commit now?"

Can you think of some undesirable long-term consequences?

_____

_____

_____

What could we do instead of lying?

_____

_____

_____

In the end, the Darlings' trick didn't work anyway!

John M.: They're raising the roof in there, Andy, with at least five instruments. Now, the law says one occupant to a single room
Andy: I know who they are. I warned them earlier today on a 907.
John: Hat in the horse trough, hey?

That might have convinced many of us, but Briscoe was committed to his own freestyle approach to lodging. . .And Charlene became more and more bold in her advances toward Andy—so much so that she required her father's constant attention.

"Ye jist had to egg her on, didn't ye?"

What was Briscoe's reaction when he finally lost control of Charlene's impulses and found her hugging Andy?

_____

_____

Blessed are the pure in heart, For they shall see God.

Matthew 5:8

All's Well that Ends Well?

As in every good sitcom, the problem's solved by the end of the program. Charlene has a good man, Andy's off the hook, and Briscoe can relax. But we know that's not real life. Many times we miss God's gift by chasing after something "better" and then blame Him when it doesn't make us happy.

Can you recall a time in your own life when you got something you <u>wanted</u> only to find that it wasn't what you <u>needed</u>?

_____

_____

_____

Do you think self-control leads to a happier ending than following our own desires?   ❏ **Yes**   ❏ **No**   ❏ **Maybe**
Why or why not?

_____

_____

The answer to our problem is found in Philippians 4:8 (see sidebar). Rather than trying to "beat the system" and find our own road to happiness, we can focus on God's truth. Self-control is a fruit of His Spirit.

GALATIANS 5:22-23
But the fruit of the Spirit is love, joy, peace, longsuffering, kindness, goodness, faithfulness, gentleness, self-control. Against such there is no law.

"The letters ye wrote me. . ."

Self-control Litmus Test

Read aloud and briefly discuss each quote below. Check the appropriate box, noting how each applies to your own personal life experience.

Little progress can be made merely by attempting to repress what is evil, our great hope lies in developing what is good.
—Calvin Coolidge[4]

❑ Applies   ❑ Sometimes Applies   ❑ Does Not Apply

The wealthy person is the one who's content with what he has.[5]
❑ Applies   ❑ Sometimes Applies   ❑ Does Not Apply

If you would learn self-mastery, begin by yielding yourself to the One Great Master.
—Johann Friedrich Lobstein[6]

❑ Applies   ❑ Sometimes Applies   ❑ Does Not Apply

Remember that throughout life pain is inevitable but misery is optional.[7]
❑ Applies   ❑ Sometimes Applies   ❑ Does Not Apply

Ever notice, it's easier to control your temper if the other guy is bigger?[8]
❑ Applies   ❑ Sometimes Applies   ❑ Does Not Apply

Take care of your reputation. It's your most valuable asset.[9]
❑ Applies   ❑ Sometimes Applies   ❑ Does Not Apply

Acquire things the old-fashioned way: Save for them and pay cash.[10]
❑ Applies   ❑ Sometimes Applies   ❑ Does Not Apply

See problems as opportunities for growth and self-mastery.[11]
❑ Applies   ❑ Sometimes Applies   ❑ Does Not Apply

Don't major in minor things.[12]
❑ Applies   ❑ Sometimes Applies   ❑ Does Not Apply

You cannot always control circumstances. But you can control your own thoughts.
—Charles E. Popplestone[13]

❑ Applies   ❑ Sometimes Applies   ❑ Does Not Apply

---

*1. **Which of the above quotes is closest to your own idea of self-control? Why?***

_____

_____

_____

2. Which presents the greatest challenge to you? Why?

_____

_____

_____

Self-control Action Points

1. Live beneath your means.
2. Make a list of ten guiding principles that you want most to direct your life. Every month or so ask your family or a friend how well you're living up to them.
3. Determine your response to temptation long before it taps you on the shoulder.
4. Form good habits. They are as hard to break as bad ones.
5. Bad things happen in bad places. So stay out of bad places.
6. Take charge of your attitude. Don't let someone else choose it for you.
7. Take your dog to obedience school. You'll both learn a lot.

Personal Notes

_____

_____

_____

_____

_____

_____

_____

_____

_____

_____

_____

_____

_____

_____

Personal Notes

[1] John Cook, *The Book of Positive Quotations* (Minneapolis: Fairview Press, 1997)

[2] *Ibid.*

[3] H. Jackson Brown, Jr., *Life's Instructions for Wisdom, Success, and Happiness* (Nashville: Rutledge Hill Press, 2000)

[4] *Ibid.*

[5] *Ibid.*

[6] Frank S. Mead, *12,000 Inspirational Quotations* (Springfield, MA: Federal Street Press, 1965)

[7] Jackson Brown, Jr., Paula Y. Flautt, and Kim Shea, *A Book of Love for My Daughter* (Nashville: Rutledge Hill Press, 2001)

[8] Lowell D. Streiker, *Nelson's Big Book of Laughter* (Nashville: Thomas Nelson, 2000)

[9] H. Jackson Brown, Jr. and Hy Brett, *A Book of Love for My Son* (Nashville: Rutledge Hill Press, 2001)

[10] *Ibid.*

[11] *Ibid.*

[12] *Ibid.*

[13] Peggy M. Anderson, *Attitude is Everything* (Lombard, IL: Successories Publishing, 1995)

Parables from The Fishin' Hole

Volume 2

Session Three
The Mountain Wedding

The Mountain Wedding
(A Study on Patience)

GALATIANS 6:9
And let us not grow weary while doing good, for in due season we shall reap if we do not lose heart.

We all look to Job as a classic model of patience in the Bible. Job endured financial ruin, loss of family, chronic illness, and public ridicule, but he still kept his faith in God. Few of us will have the troubles of Job. But none of us can escape the trials of dealing with folks who just don't see things the way we do. That's when our patience is really tested.

The Mountain Wedding gives us a golden opportunity to consider someone totally obstinate and learn how to win him over—with patience. Earnest T. Bass is a strange fellow, but he is not someone you can just ignore!

How would you define the word "patience"?

_____

_____

_____

_____

Do you consider yourself a patient person?
☐ **Yes**   ☐ **No**   ☐ **Maybe**   *Why or why not?*

_____

_____

> He that can have patience can have what he will.
>
> —**Benjamin Franklin**[1]

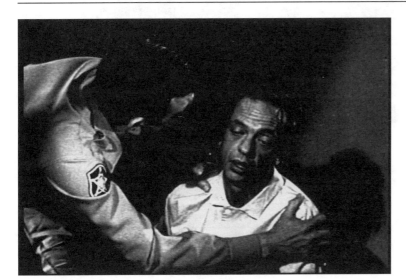

"I'm awake. . ."

Enter "The Villain"

Maybe we meet him at work. Maybe she's a classmate or roomie. Even in-laws can qualify. Sooner or later, we can be sure that we'll find someone who grinds us the wrong way—constantly. Earnest T. Bass definitely pressed the Darlings' envelope for tolerance.

Andy: You say you got trouble?
Briscoe: It's a sight.
Andy: Well, what in the world's the matter?
Briscoe: Well, they's this fella, Earnest T. Bass. He just don't take to Dud and Charlene being' married.
Andy: Well, it's all legal 'n everything. I give you a copy of the marriage certificate and kept a copy here for my files.
Briscoe: I know that. But that don't signify with Earnest T. Bass. He keeps botherin' Charlene—yellin' in the night, throwin' rocks through the windows.
Andy: Can't you and your boys handle him?
Briscoe: Well, we thought about killin' him. Kinda hated to go that far.
Barney: It's a wise man that knows it's illegal to take the law into his own hands.
Briscoe (to Andy) He arguin' with me?
Andy: He's agreeing with you.
Briscoe: Just so's I know where I stand.

"Leave the gun be, mister."

What made Earnest T. Bass so difficult to endure?

_____

_____

Do you know anyone who acts like him? In what way? (No names, please.)

_____

_____

.

28

"They all keyed up."

Begin at the Beginning

It was clear from the start that Earnest T. Bass was not your average neighbor!

Briscoe: Did you tell Earnest T. Bass the sheriff was lookin' fer 'im?
Dud: I couldn't find him, Mr. Darling. His cousin said he went off into the woods to kill a mockingbird
Andy: That don't sound like a very nice person.
Briscoe: One of the worst we got.
Andy: Maybe Barney and I ought to go out and look for 'im.
Dudley: Oh, he a pestilence, and a pestilence will find you. You just wait. He'll be along.

But still, Andy tried first to work things out on the rational level.

Andy: Now look here, Mr. Bass. I'm the Justice of the Peace in Mayberry. I married Charlene and Dud and I've got a copy of the marriage certificate here to prove it.
Earnest T. Bass: You a preacher?
Andy: No.
E.T. Bass: Then they ain't rightly married. Now I got a chance to sweet talk and woo and charm her with my ways.
Briscoe: Take a shot at 'im, Sheriff. You got a legal right.

Why do you think Andy tried to reason with Earnest T. when everyone who knew E.T.B. said that he would not listen to reason?

_____

_____

_____

Patience serves as a protection against wrongs as clothes do against cold. For if you put on more clothes as the cold increases it will have no power to hurt you. So in like manner you must grow in patience when you meet with great wrongs, and they will then be powerless to vex your mind.

–Leonardo Da Vinci[2]

When facing a difficult task, act as though it is impossible to fail. If you're going after Moby Dick, take along the tartar sauce.[3]

Have you ever skipped this step when trying to resolve a disagreement? If so, what happened?

_____

_____

_____

_____

But when Andy met Earnest T. Bass for himself and watched him cavort through the woods waving a gun, he came to a deeper understanding of the problem.

Andy: If you ask me, this Earnest T. Bass is a strange and weird character.
Briscoe: Just plan ornery is what he is.
Barney: I think he's a nut!

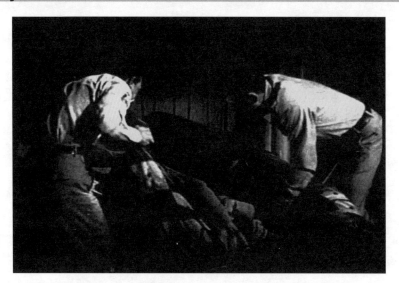

"Do you suppose it'd help if we turned 'em over?"

The best strategy now was to wait for E.T.B. to make the next move and "catch him in the act." Predictably, it came in the middle of the night, beginning with a rock through the window. Everyone was awake in a flash. Understandably, their next reaction was *anger*.

Briscoe: Earnest T. Bass, . . . You're a low-down, pesky buzzard. Doggone ya!
E. T. B.: Sticks and stones may break my bones, but names cain't niver touch me!
Andy: Earnest T. Bass, you better quit throwin' rocks through this winda. I'm gonna have to arrest you if you don't go on home. You're disturbing the peace, keeping these folks awake.
E.T.B.: Well, tell 'em all to go to sleep. It's just Charlene I want to talk to.

Have you ever tried to convince someone to change their behavior by responding to them with anger? ❏ **Yes** ❏ **No** ❏ **Often**
If so, what was the result?

_____

_____

_____

When another stone flew through the window, Barney took the next step: hotter anger, bigger threats!

Barney: You listen to me out there! This is Deputy Fife speakin' and I'm armed. And if you don't go away, I'm just liable to take a shot out this winda! *(E.T.B. throws stone through window.)*
Barney: You cut that out! *(Stone comes through another window.)*
Briscoe (to Andy): You better stop that deputy of yours. He'll get us stoned to death!

Yes, it's funny when Barney does it. But you've done it too, haven't you? ❏ **Yes**   ❏ **No**   ❏ **Often**

Did it work (for more than a day or two)?

_____

_____

_____

Finally, Earnest T. Bass drives Andy to the ultimate weapon: patience.

Barney: What are you gonna do, Andy.
Andy: Only one thing to do. Have him speak his piece and maybe he'll go on home. Charlene, come on over here and let him talk to you. Maybe he'll get it out of his system.

"Fire too hot, jump in the pot. . ."

When you get to the end of your rope, tie a knot and hang on.

−**Franklin D. Roosevelt**[4]

31

Not only does Andy use patience, but he helps the Darlings be patient too—first Darlene, then Dudley, then Briscoe.

Bend with the Wind

JAMES 1:19
So then, my beloved brethren, let every man be swift to hear, slow to speak, slow to wrath.

The force of a strong wind can fell a sturdy but rigid oak easier than a supple willow that bends with the wind. Andy did not ignore Earnest T. Bass' threats, but he did not meet them head on, either. Instead, he devised a plan that allowed Earnest to save face at the same time Dud and Charlene had their church wedding.

For the plan to work, Dudley and Charlene also had to modify their plans. Charlene also had to give up the pleasure of wearing her wedding gown to achieve the greater goal.

Do you have a situation that requires you to be flexible before it can be resolved?   ❑ **Yes**   ❑ **No**
If so, what will you need to do so you can bend with the wind instead of being toppled?

_____

_____

_____

_____

A wrathful man stirs up strife, But *he who is slow to anger* allays contention.

Proverbs 15:18

"Ye look jist like yer maw."

PATIENCE LITMUS TEST

Read aloud and briefly discuss each quote below. Check the appropriate box, noting how each applies to your own personal life experience.

The art of being wise is the art of knowing what to overlook.   –William James[5]
❑ Applies   ❑ Sometimes Applies   ❑ Does Not Apply

Some people just can't enjoy life; the first half of their lives are spent blaming their troubles on their parents and the second half on their children.   –Rev. Denis R. Fakes[6]
❑ Applies   ❑ Sometimes Applies   ❑ Does Not Apply

Remember that overnight success usually takes about fifteen years.[7]
❑ Applies   ❑ Sometimes Applies   ❑ Does Not Apply

Be willing to lose a battle in order to win the war.[8]
❑ Applies   ❑ Sometimes Applies   ❑ Does Not Apply

We're not primarily put on this earth to see through one another, but to see one another through.   –Peter De Vries[9]
❑ Applies   ❑ Sometimes Applies   ❑ Does Not Apply

Life is a lot like a high-school algebra class. Every time you get one problem solved, the teacher is waiting to give you another.[10]
❑ Applies   ❑ Sometimes Applies   ❑ Does Not Apply

---

1. *Which of the above quotes is closest to your own idea of patience? Why?*

_____

_____

_____

2. *Which presents the greatest challenge to you? Why?*

_____

_____

_____

_____

Patience Action Points

1. Remember that children need loving the most when they are the hardest to love.
2. When you've decided to give up on something or someone, give it just one more try
3. Don't tailgate.
4. Never give a loved one a gift that suggests they need improvement.

Personal Notes

_____

_____

_____

_____

_____

_____

_____

_____

_____

_____

_____

_____

_____

_____

_____

_____

_____

_____

_____

_____

_____

_____

Personal Notes

[1] Rudolf Flesch, *The New Book of Unusual Quotations* (New York: Harper & Row, 1966)

[2] *Ibid.*

[3] H. Jackson Brown, Jr. and Hy Brett, *A Book of Love for My Son* (Nashville: Rutledge Hill Press, 2001)

[4] Peggy M. Anderson, *Attitude is Everything* (Lombard, IL: Successories Publishing, 1995)

[5] H. Jackson Brown, Jr., *Life's Instructions for Wisdom, Success, and Happiness* (Nashville: Rutledge Hill Press, 2000)

[6] Lowell D. Streiker, *Nelson's Big Book of Laughter* (Nashville: Thomas Nelson, 2000)

[7] H. Jackson Brown, Jr. and Hy Brett, *A Book of Love for My Son* (Nashville: Rutledge Hill Press, 2001)

[8] *Ibid.*

[9] Lowell D. Streiker, *Nelson's Big Book of Laughter* (Nashville: Thomas Nelson, 2000)

[10] *Ibid.*

Parables from The Fishin' Hole

Volume 2

Session Four
Rafe Hollister Sings

Rafe Hollister Sings
(A Study on Forbearance)

LUKE 6:29

To him who strikes you on the one cheek, offer the other also. And from him who takes away your cloak, do not withhold your tunic either.

What happens when someone refuses to retaliate for an injury—a slap on the face or the snatching of a coat? The Civil Rights Movement of the '60s is one of history's examples. Passive resistance to violence brought down the iron walls of segregation. If you've ever met a person with such strong character, you will not soon forget them. Rafe Hollister is just this kind of folk and he wins the praise of the whole town of Mayberry by staying true to himself.

How would you define the word "forbearance"?

_____

_____

_____

Do you think forbearance is possible in today's violent culture?
❏ **Yes**   ❏ **No**   ❏ **Unsure**   *Why or why not?*

_____

_____

_____

The discretion of a man makes him slow to anger,
And his glory *is* to overlook a transgression.

Proverbs 19:11

"Believe me, if all those endearing young charms. . ."

A Gift Unwrapped

Apparently, no one knew that Rafe could sing until he overheard Barney murdering the song, "Believe Me, If All Those Endearing Young Charms". He gently offers his observation:

Rafe: I don't mean to butt in, but that's not how it goes.
Andy: It's a good thing you showed up here, Rafe. Why don't you join along and sing with Barn. You don't mind do you, Barn?
Barney: Well, no. It'll be a little tough for you to keep up, Rafe, but sing along as best you can. Sing along with Barn.

Would you have taken offense at Barney's mistaken belief that he was better than you were? ❑ **Yes** ❑ **No** ❑ **Maybe**
Why or why not?

_____

_____

"What would you do if they asked you to sing a cappella?"

When Rafe proved that he could really sing, Barney worked harder to put him down. Again, Rafe shows amazing restraint. Instead of reacting to Barney's insults, he appears confident in his own ability and decides to put it to the test at the Musicale tryouts.

Andy: Why don't you take Rafe over there and have him sing for 'em.
Barney: You want Rafe to be embarrassed and humiliated. They want people up there with musical backgrounds. That don't mean you have to stop singing, Rafe. You just go ahead and do it. You sing in the bathtub, don't you? Well, you go right ahead and do that.
Rafe: Can I ask a question? What time are these here tryouts?
Andy: Well, I don't know. Why?
Rafe: Well, I reckon since they ain't never around when I'm taking a bath, I best go on over there.

If someone obviously insults you, how do you react? Do you let them rule your behavior or do you maintain your belief in yourself?

_____

_____

Do you think it is harder to "keep your cool" when someone else overhears the insults?   ❑ **Yes**   ❑ **No**   ❑ **Maybe**
Why or why not?

_____

_____

_____

Rafe did have someone staunchly supporting him—John Masters, the music director.

John Masters: So genuine. A fully natural feeling. A perfect pitch. Yes. Amazing he's kept it to himself all this time. Mayberry is going to have a representative we can all be proud of at the Musicale.

If someone compliments you on the heels of another's insults, which person are you inclined to believe?

_____

_____

_____

How might your above choice affect your behavior? Why?

_____

_____

"The way he dresses!"

He who has not forgiven an enemy has never yet tasted one of the most sublime enjoyments of life.

–Johann Kaspar Lavater[2]

The Attack Widens

Barney's unkind comments were probably based on jealousy and insecurity. That makes them fairly easy to dismiss. But what happens next to Rafe is mean-spirited opposition.

Mayor Stoner: What is this? Some kind of joke you're pulling? John Masters was just in here and he told us the choice for the musicale: Rafe Hollister! You want Rafe Hollister to represent us at the musicale. I understand this was your idea.
Andy: No, I just suggested he go up there and sing, but John Masters picked him fair and square. What's wrong with Rafe singing, anyway?
Mayor: What's *wrong?!!*
Mrs. Jeffries: Sheriff, you must face the facts. Rafe Hollister is simply not presentable. The way he dresses! And to present him at *my* organization—a club that has been dedicated to the finer things in life? Never!
Andy: Rafe's already been told he won.
Mayor: You make it clear to him that he will not be representing the fair city of Mayberry!

Andy is outraged at the unfair decision of Mayor Stoner and Mrs. Jeffries, but he gives in to their pressure when he goes to Rafe's farm to tell him he can't sing.

Can you think of another way Andy might have handled their objections?

_____

_____

When Andy sees Rafe's and Martha's excitement about the Musicale, he doesn't have the heart to tell Rafe he can't sing. But when he sees Rafe's "Sunday best" Andy has second thoughts.

"How do I look?"

Andy: Boy, I'm in trouble. If he shows up at the Musicale looking like that, Mayor and Mrs. Jeffries will have a fit! I guess we'll have to go out and get him some clothes.

Who was Andy really helping when he tried to trick Rafe into wearing an ill-fitting new suit? Why?

_____

_____

But even that doesn't satisfy the Mayor and Mrs. Jeffries. They reveal the depth of their disdain when they come to check up on Rafe at practice.

"I'd rather spend another ten days in jail."

Andy: Rafe does look nice, don't he?
Mayor Stoner: Well, I don't know . . .
Mrs. Jeffries: Oh, I suppose he looks good enough to get by. It'll be all right as long as he doesn't associate with anyone.
Mayor Stoner: Yes, you see to that, Sheriff.

Their attitudes were obvious to Martha, overhearing their comments to Andy. Although she says nothing, Andy sees the hurt on her face and recognizes how wrong he has been in trying to please the Mayor.

Do you think Rafe would have behaved differently if he knew what the Mayor and Mrs. Jeffries had said?

_____

_____

_____

Don't expect life to be fair.

A Win-Win-Win-Lose Finale

1 CORINTHIANS 13:4-7

Love suffers long and is kind; love does not envy; love does not parade itself, is not puffed up; does not behave rudely, does not seek its own, is not provoked, thinks no evil; does not rejoice in iniquity, but rejoices in the truth; bears all things, believes all things, hopes all things, endures all things.

Mrs. Dennis: What a perfectly marvelous idea to have him appear dressed that way. It made his selection so much more authentic. Mr. Hollister, will you favor us with another selection?

If we read between the lines, we can safely guess that Andy advised Rafe in reaching the right balance in his appearance.

In the end, Rafe wins because he had the joy of performing at the Musicale and didn't give in to resentment because of the way he was treated. Andy wins because he helped Rafe succeed. The audience wins because they heard a beautiful program.

Only Mayor Stoner and Mrs. Jeffries lost because they refused to see Rafe's true worth.

FORBEARANCE LITMUS TEST

Read aloud and briefly discuss each quote below. Check the appropriate box, noting how each applies to your own personal life experience.

There's no point in burying a hatchet if you're going to put up a marker on the site.

–Sydney Harris[5]

❑ Applies   ❑ Sometimes Applies   ❑ Does Not Apply

Almost any event will put on a new face when received with cheerful acceptance.

–Henry S. Haskins[6]

❑ Applies   ❑ Sometimes Applies   ❑ Does Not Apply

Being too quick to judge someone can deprive you of a great encounter and the possibility of a wonderful long-term relationship.[7]

❑ Applies   ❑ Sometimes Applies   ❑ Does Not Apply

It is easier for the generous to forgive, than for the offender to ask forgiveness.

–James Thomson[8]

Remember that all happy marriages are the result of compromising and forgiving.[9]

❑ Applies   ❑ Sometimes Applies   ❑ Does Not Apply

Never underestimate the power of a kind word or deed.[10]

❑ Applies   ❑ Sometimes Applies   ❑ Does Not Apply

Understand that happiness is not based on possessions, power, or prestige, but on relationships with people you love and respect.[11]

❑ Applies   ❑ Sometimes Applies   ❑ Does Not Apply

---

1. Which of the above quotes is closest to your own idea of forbearance? Why?

_____

_____

_____

2. Which presents the greatest challenge to you? Why?

_____

_____

_____

Forbearance Action Points

1. Take time to get to know people. Resist the temptation to judge them by how they look or what they wear.
2. If you can't forgive and forget, you can at least forgive and move on.
3. Laugh a lot. A good sense of humor cures almost all of life's ills.[12]
4. Don't allow self-pity. The moment this emotion strikes, do something nice for someone less fortunate than you.
5. When you have been wronged, a poor memory is your best response.

Personal Notes

_____

_____

_____

_____

_____

_____

_____

_____

_____

_____

_____

_____

_____

_____

_____

_____

_____

_____

_____

_____

_____

Personal Notes

[1] H. Jackson Brown, Jr., *Life's Instructions for Wisdom, Success, and Happiness* (Nashville: Rutledge Hill Press, 2000)
[2] Frank S. Mead, *12,000 Inspirational Quotations* (Springfield, MA: Federal Street Press, 1965)
[3] Frank S. Mead, *12,000 Inspirational Quotations* (Springfield, MA: Federal Street Press, 1965)
[4] H. Jackson Brown, Jr. and Hy Brett, *A Book of Love for My Son* (Nashville: Rutledge Hill Press, 2001)
[5] John Cook, *The Book of Positive Quotations* (Minneapolis: Fairview Press, 1997)
[6] John Cook, *The Book of Positive Quotations* (Minneapolis: Fairview Press, 1997)
[7] H. Jackson Brown, Jr., *Life's Instructions for Wisdom, Success, and Happiness* (Nashville: Rutledge Hill Press, 2000)
[8] Frank S. Mead, *12,000 Inspirational Quotations* (Springfield, MA: Federal Street Press, 1965)
[9] Jackson Brown, Jr., Paula Y. Flautt, and Kim Shea, *A Book of Love for My Daughter* (Nashville: Rutledge Hill Press, 2001)
[10] H. Jackson Brown, Jr. and Hy Brett, *A Book of Love for My Son* (Nashville: Rutledge Hill Press, 2001)
[11] H. Jackson Brown, Jr. and Hy Brett, *A Book of Love for My Son* (Nashville: Rutledge Hill Press, 2001)
[12] H. Jackson Brown, Jr. and Hy Brett, *A Book of Love for My Son* (Nashville: Rutledge Hill Press, 2001)